Artistic Table Setting

ARTISTIC
TABLE SETTING

PHOTOGRAPHS BY MASSIMO LISTRI

FORWARD BY CRISTINA ACIDINI LUCHINAT

IDEA BOOKS

Special thanks to architect Ettore Mucchetti
editor of AD - Le più belle case del mondo
for his unfailing helpfulness

© IdeArte srl, Milano
Idea Books - via Regia, 53
55049 Viareggio
info@ideabooks.com - www.ideabooks.com

© Photographs by Massimo Listri

Editorial staff: Nicoletta del Buono and Federica Clari
Graphics: Marco de Sensi
Image processing: Andrea Dalle Luche

Photo credits:
pages 8, 10-11, 13, 14, 17 Archivo Fotografico SCALA, Firenze

ISBN 88 88033 58 7
10 9 8 7 6 5 4 3 2 1

Printed in China

Summary

Theatres of Taste

The cultural and symbolic function of food and drink served at table finds knowledgeable people in quite different fields in agreement, ranging from Claude Lévy-Strauss, a father of anthropology, to Pellegrino Artusi, author of *La scienza in cucina e l'arte di mangiar bene* (1891), the renowned treatise on gastronomy constituting a milestone in the history of traditional Italian cuisine. Not by chance, two towering figures of Western culture wrote texts with titles deriving from a situation where food and drink are shared: Plato with his *Symposium* and Dante with the *Banquet*. The elaboration of nutritional substances, in differentiating us from animals, characterises us as human beings; the giddy variety of ingredients and processes involved culminates at the time of consumption when food and drink is served at table, whether a solitary meal or sumptuous banquet.

The table is precisely what the extraordinary sampling of pictures contained in this book is devoted to. Taken in a wide variety of countries around the world by Massimo Listri with his infallible eye and equally infallible photographic equipment, the skill of the shots, perfection of the light, and harmonious warmth and coolness of the colours make every photograph a silent tale with a different protagonist: now we have the suspended poetry of an exotic environment with sand and palms; now the precious evidence of objects; now the triumphant vitality of fruit and vegetables; now the quiet solemnity of a room that is practically a museum – and yet more.

But all of them capture the *genius loci*, the stylistic signature of the masters of the house, whom we imagine on tiptoe in back of the photographer, excluded from the earthly paradises arranged by them, where the only living creature admitted, if any, is the cat. And here is exactly where the magic of the set of tables presented here lies: the crystalline and motionless perfection of the moment preceding the entry of human beings to officiate the rite of the meal, the authentic essence of the *still life*, as English speakers express so beautifully the more abstract and gloomy Italian term *natura morta*. Every table is conceived as an ephemeral masterwork that the table companions will throw into disorder – which is

Left: Domenico Ghirlandaio (1449-1494), Last Supper, detail, Church of Ognissanti, Florence.

their role – in the end leaving tumultuous scenes of leftovers and used tableware, which in the past certain Flemish painters, whose insatiable curiosity to investigate reality stopped at nothing, went so far as to reproduce. They did this so effectively that for a while a picture called *After Dinner* was attributed to the great Caravaggio by the great Roberto Longhi: "The unconsumed 'after dinner': the carafe half empty, the watermelon and melon sliced, the apple intact and half a pear, the flies jumping over their own shadow…" (Roberto Longhi, *Caravaggio*, Editori Riuniti, Rome, 1968).

But in Listri's tables – or rather those of the community of friends who opened their doors to him for the joy of our eyes – consumption and disorder are far away, banished, impossible. It does not occur to us to ask ourselves whether the bread is still fresh or how long the cut flowers will last. *"Là, tout n'est qu'ordre et beauté, / Luxe, calme et volupté,"* we might comment with Baudelaire, transported in interiors of different types of beauty, with the same pleasure of amazed children when, marching along a runner or shuffling in our prescribed felt slippers, we admire the long set tables of residences and castles from Eastern to Western Europe. Theatres that are a feast for the eyes anticipate and postpone the pleasures of the other senses: the tastes and smells, the voices and music, the smooth contact with linens and damasks, glasses and cutlery cool to the touch, the domestic asperity of the bread that we are given to break by hand, as in an archaic and timeless ceremony.

Art and prose have handed down treasures of the imagination and knowledge of the table settings of the past, beginning from the tables of Graeco-Roman myth, Christian religion and Western literature. In the extraordinary artistic flowering of Rome in the early sixteenth century, in the splendid age of Julius II and Leo X, artists were fond of imagining *The Banquet of the Gods* on Mount Olympus as a

Below: Stefano d'Antonio Vanni (1407-1483), Last Supper, Sant'Andrea a Cercina, Florence.

sumptuous court fête, with embossed tableware of gold and silver, fabulous cups, specially arranged furniture with "sideboards for special occasions" or entire dinner services of pottery or metal or glass, lined up on shelves for sheer show. And apropos of sideboards for special occasions – a rare present-day specimen of which appears with the function of *eye-catcher* in one of Listri's masterly shots – it comes as no surprise that huge sums and creative resources were lavished, beginning from the Renaissance, for these extremely valuable dinner services.

The potters of the Duchy of Urbino were specialised in a type of production featuring pieces painted with scenes from history or myth. Used for dowries, presented to the powerful, purloined in wartime and looting, they included countless different objects: coolers, hand basins, plates, cups, stands and trays, often richly decorated as described above to display not only the owner's wealth but also his cultural bent. A refined show in Écouen, *Le dressoir du prince: services d'apparat à la Renaissance* (catalogue edited by Éditions des Musées Nationaux, Paris, 1995) had the merit of gathering items of spectacular beauty and rarity scattered in different museums, which conjured up noble purchasers throughout Europe: Anne of Brittany, Isabella d'Este, Catherine de' Medici, Albert V of Bavaria … and the sideboards of the Medici and Farnese families were missing.

The High Renaissance is the age when the variety of the furnishings for the table or dining room became most exuberant and fanciful: this was a time of proliferation of amphorae and coolers of considerable size, while cups and flasks of precious rock crystal, thought to be petrified ice, appeared on court tables for serving chilled beverages with spectacular elegance. Even the shapes and materials of the humble saltcellar multiplied as never before; it is not by chance that the loveliest saltcellar in the

world, fashioned by Benvenuto Cellini for Francis I of France, dates from the sixteenth century. When wood, lead, gold, silver and glass were joined first by ceramics and then porcelain, the shapes rapidly expanded, with saltcellars becoming round, oval, ships, urns, triangular, cubes, towers, balustrades, tiered and with multiple spice holders (G. Bernasconi, editor, *Saliere dal XVI al XIX secolo*, Milan, 2005). The worldly splendour of the aristocratic banquets was depicted in paintings with biblical and evangelical subjects, where the whole weight of iconography permitted or rather imposed it: the banquets of Belshazzar, Absalom, Ester and Ahasuerus, Herod and the wedding of Cana.

Greater simplicity or rather austerity were required for scenes devoted to the meals shared by Jesus with the Apostles and disciples: in the home of Simon, Martha and Mary, and Levi, in Emmaus and, naturally, *The Last Supper*, a subject very frequent in easel and wall painting, often found in the refectories of religious communities, which in Central Italy take the name *cenacolo*, indicating at once the large room and the characteristic painting. A quantity of information is gleaned from versions of *The Last Supper* painted from the fourteenth century to the early seventeenth century.

The whiteness of the tablecloth, sometimes underlined by simple hems, is modulated by pleats and drapes and at times by the regular chequered pattern, all telling a tale of hot irons, clever hands and table linen stacked in closets. The tableware is earthenware and glass in the oldest examples, but beginning from the late fifteenth century trays, hand basins and amphorae of shiny embossed metal make their appearance. The archaic custom of two people eating off the same chopping board and drinking from the same glass disappears, supplanted by the modern table laid with individual place settings. The cutlery is still essential and unchanged from olden times: the knife for solid foods and spoon for soups. It is only right to mention the religious symbolism attached to the foods scattered around the table. The bread and wine are obviously associated with Eucharist and roast lamb stands for the sacrifice of the innocent, while the salt and water remind us of baptism (C. Acidini Luchinat and R. Caterina Proto Pisani, editors, *La tradizione fiorentina dei Cenacoli*, Florence, 1997).

The table of *The Last Supper* is therefore austere, with the only possible luxury being a handful of cherries and some other fruit. But in times of exuberant narrative splendour there were those who departed from the rules imposed by historical and doctrinal plausibility, which the precepts springing from the Council of Trent (1542-63) had made more severe. And so it was that in 1573 Paolo Caliari, known as

Right: Filippo Lippi (1406-1469), Life of St John the Baptist, detail of Banquet of Herod, Duomo, Prato.

Veronese, found himself having to answer before the Tribunal of the Inquisition for having depicted in his huge *Last Supper* executed for the church of SS. Giovanni e Paolo (5.55 x 12.80 metres, now in the Louvre in Paris) a scene of unheard grandiosity, crammed with personalities and particulars not found in the biblical account: portraits of living persons, servants, dogs, "buffoons, drunks, Germans, dwarfs and similar scurrilities." Veronese put forward the reasons of variety and richness in art, adding in his defence, "We painters take the licence that poets and madmen take," a colloquial version of the *fingendi aequa potestas* that Horace earlier claimed for painters and poets. And so the busy *Last Supper* was forced to undergo a transformation, by the hand of Veronese himself, into *Dinner at the House of Levi – likewise a biblical* event, but devoid of the supreme sacredness associated with the Eucharist in the Last Supper. Together with the tables sanctified by the presence of Christ, other tables endowed with powerful symbolic meanings make their appearance in Western culture, the most famous of which is certainly the Round Table of King Arthur and his knights.

How important is and always has been the time and manner of the breaking of bread together. This is shown among other things by the repeated warnings by authors of classics and modern authors alike to maintain an appropriate bon ton or at least decent behaviour. The oldest treatises lavish advice on the proper use of the napkin and the disposal of stripped bones, while as we approach our day we find rules of etiquette that transpose the complex aristocratic rituals of former times into a dimension of bourgeois elegance: in books of etiquette we never fail to find a chapter devoted to the table as a place where attention to aesthetics is fundamental for the host or hostess, inasmuch as what is involved is making known one's economic status and breeding.

Today's styles of laying the table mark the success of a variety of aesthetic and cultural references from which one is basically free to choose. As Renato Barilli puts it, "No less than any aesthetic experience or work of art, a meal can fall within the co-ordinates of classic, baroque, rustic, or sophisticated/decadent taste and so forth" (A. Appiano, *Bello da mangiare: il cibo come forma simbolica nell'arte*, Rome, 2000, 9). The tables photographed by Listri offer an excellent case study of this plurality.

A decision absolutely preceding any other determines the final result: whether or not to use a tablecloth. In the latter case, the table is bare except for American-style place mats, coasters and service plates at each individual place setting, perhaps to set off the lovely marble, wood or glass of the table or some

Left: Pontormo (1494-1556), Supper in Emmaus, Galleria degli Uffizi, Florence.

technological novelty. And if one decides to use a tablecloth the dizzying range of fabrics includes rustic linens, the classic damasks of Flanders, filets on "transparent" material, ethnic weaves and amber-coloured Indian gauze recently in vogue. The colour range is equally wide, from unsullied white reminiscent of grandmother's trousseau to the greys and mastic of the natural textile fibres, delicate pastels and bold hues.

In any case, only the room – and therefore the house – can govern the choices, inspiring harmonies that begin with the walls, curtains and furnishings that reverberate on the table and dinnerware. In outdoor settings it is the very nature of the place – whether it is a formal garden, rustic yard with kitchen garden, Oriental beach or rooftop terrace with a view of the urban *skyline* – that determines the aesthetic suggestions to follow.

And now, allowing ourselves enough time to satisfy our curiosity, let us begin to follow our itinerary of tables that will amaze us with their constantly changing forms, materials, colours and tints, confirming once more how objects of everyday use can fall, when skilfully combined, within the highest sphere of creativity and interpret, no less than other visual phenomena such as fashion or cinema, the atmosphere of the time. An elegant *sourtout de table*, a clever centrepiece or a composition that delights without excess are small masterpieces in themselves, dear to us even if something other than the miniature fountains of precious metal that once adorned the tables of the ancien régime. Here one thinks of the spectacular ones of the czars (illustrated by G. A. Markova in "*Silberne Kredenzen und Tafelaufsätze auf dem Zarentisch*," R. Eikelmann (ed.), *Studien zur europäischen Goldschmiedekunst des 14. bis 20. Jahrhunderts*, Munich, 2001, 131-142).

We tiptoe in, with the timid curiosity of one invited by total strangers. Like *Giovannino Senza Paura* in the dining hall of the enchanted castle, we shall find tables laid by mysterious hands awaiting equally mysterious table companions, and even foods already served and lit candles, but, unlike the hero of the tale of Tuscany, there will be no need for us to fear a giant falling down the chimney one piece at a time to disturb the supper no little. The charm captured by the lens is all in the motionless, silent life of the objects that, having come to an agreement among themselves, speak the deaf-and-dumb language of taste and harmony to our eyes and mind, suggesting to always leave a place at our table, whether neo-baroque or minimalist, for Beauty.

Right: Paolo Veronese (1528-1588), Wedding of Cana, detail, Louvre, Paris.

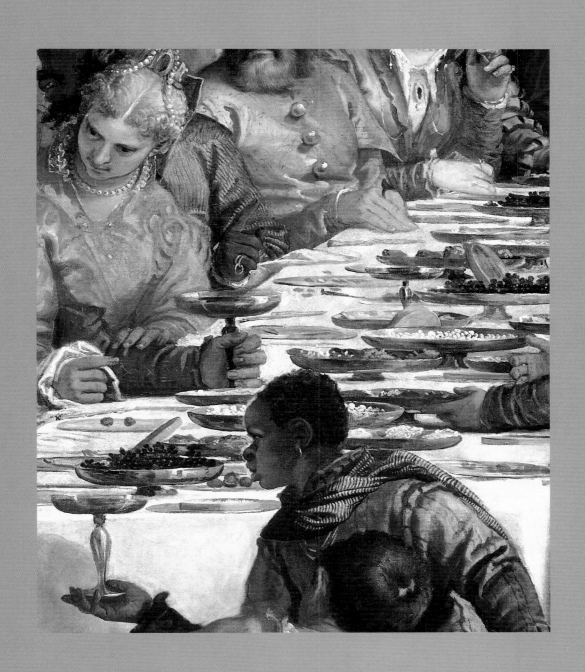

the First Ritual

Few customs divide the world's countries and civilisations like breakfast. Considering Europe alone, two basic approaches with their infinite variations are immediately recognisable: the Nordic approach, exported to the United States, which favours foods high in calories and proteins, including eggs, sausages, fish and dairy products; and the Mediterranean approach based on baked goods such as the brioche, croissant and tarts. Overlapping tastes include milk, coffee, tea and cereals. If, roughly speaking, this is the divide when it comes to food, what unites us is an aesthetic desire: to find a well-laid table upon awakening, bright with gleaming tableware and fragrant with bread fresh out of the oven.

The dream never quite comes true at home. At a good hotel it is a reality, a paradise at our disposal. But, as mentioned at the outset, the breakfast tables photographed by Listri manage to evoke magical situations that draw on rhythms and ways of bygone times, when the *petit déjeuner* had the significance of the first ritual of the day for the gathered family, perhaps assisted by the discreet and competent presence of domestics.

Visually speaking, breakfast is inspired by natural values and colours, fundamentally those of milk and bread. White or ivory porcelain services are welcome, discretely edged in gold.

Teapots, coffee pots, old silver milk jugs with warm tints, as well as stainless steel espresso pots of such smart design as to be in perfect keeping with a hi-tech table. The amber of the bread and biscuits heightens the colour of the butter, the golden honey and different hues of the jams.

Without losing in domestic intimacy, these table settings seem to invite us to begin the day under the banner of unhurried or, better yet, timeless charm.

Right, lower left: In a residence overlooking the Arno in Florence, conceived as the refuge of a cultivated European traveller of the mid-nineteenth century, the breakfast table is laid among romantic Grand Tour souvenirs, in front of a nineteenth-century sofa of ebony inlaid with ivory and covered with horsehair. A late eighteenth-century Burmese silver and copper teapot embossed by hand stands out on the small nineteenth-century table.

The wall is hung with two oval temperas illustrating jewellery designs by Fabergé for an Indian customer and a set of watercolours depicting late-nineteenth-century Indian persons of rank. Oriental and Western touches intermingle in a dreamy atmosphere of memories, stylistic and historicist oddities, literary borrowings and riveting narrative flows.

Below right: Cherries, candied fruit, a basket of strawberry tree fruits: everything necessary for preparing a rich Mediterranean breakfast based on sweets and fresh and dried fruit. The only salted item finds a small salt cellar and eggcup of white porcelain for enjoying hard- or soft-boiled eggs with a pinch of salt.

In pure French style, the Jacquard tablecloth and napkins feature sunny hues.

Left: Breakfast in the kitchen passes muster if the taste is neo-classic and Mediterranean. On a walnut table from the Region of Liguria and below a French trompe-l'œil panel, both dating from the early nineteenth century, biscuits, fragrant bread, café-au-lait and home-made jams are served among silver, crystal and earthenware by Giustiniani, the famous Neapolitan factory.

Right: A few steps from Goethe's home cum museum in Rome, in an apartment brightened by evocative art objects and precious souvenirs of the Grand Tour, the kitchen table is laid for breakfast in a setting of light wainscot and grisailles of the eighteenth century that seems borrowed from *The Return of Casanova* by Arthur Schnitzler or a film by James Ivory. A small pickled table edged in gold leaf is laid with crystal and *pâte de verre* cups in front of a dresser with truncated tympanum on which is placed an eighteenth-century grisaille. Emphasising the play of the blacks and whites, two cushions resting on the small white Gustav III seats are embroidered with the profiles of Roman emperors.

Above: In the Engadine home of Maria Luisa Trussardi, breakfast is consumed even in the wintertime – at least on nice days – on the terrace with southern exposure on the Lake of St. Moritz, sheltered from the chill north winds. The violet plates with gold trim are by Trussardi, as are the glasses with satiny circular decorations. In the middle of the table there is no lack of sliced Sacher torte and the typical Nusstorte of the Engadine area. Then there is dark rye bread and Bundnerfleish, the cured meat of the Grisons similar to the *bresaola* of Valtellina but with a more delicate flavour, served with sweet and sour gherkins.

Right: The first meal of the day in the country: before the large fireplace with stone cornice, surmounted by decorative plates by Vecchia Lodi, cereals, biscuits, tea and coffee are served with a solid silver Art Deco teapot and coffee pot: a suggestive compromise between a Mediterranean breakfast based on sweets, fruit and café-au-lait, and a Continental or English breakfast with eggs and Cornflakes.

Above: Chequered tablecloth and rustic earthenware with floral motifs make for an Italian-style breakfast, served in a farmhouse in the hills of the Chianti district, exactly where Bernardo Bertolucci shot the most suggestive scenes of *I Dance Alone*. In this stone house furnished with peasant furniture even the table decorations and the plain, genuine foods bespeak useful and industrious lives in a rural language of yesteryear in harmony with the *genius loci*.

Left: Neapolitan-style coffee prepared with the traditional coffee pot that is overturned, served on Capri before the dazzling panorama of the Faraglioni cliffs, in an atmosphere of cultivated, intelligent leisure in keeping with the nature of the favourite island of the emperor Tiberius. The porcelain coffee cups are arranged on a habillé table, surrounded by small low Moroccan armchairs of hammered silver that emphasise the Mediterranean note of this sunny scene.

Following pages: A London house on the Thames. In front of the ample sets of English-style windows and under an old adjustable lamp, a nineteenth-century table is laid for breakfast in pure British style: orange juice, fresh fruit salad, eggs, toast with orange marmalade and, obviously, tea. The chinaware rests on American-style place mats; the table is left uncovered, as is the custom in English-speaking countries.

A palazzo of Cortina d'Ampezzo, furnished as a sort of *Wunderkammer*, brings back the charms of the patrician mountain residences of the late Hapsburg era. The small dining room, facing the town hall of Cortina with its windows with illusionist decorations, is where all the meals are consumed, including breakfast. Here the lovely light and dark walnut table inlaid with hunting scenes in ivory, a late eighteenth-century Austrian masterpiece, is laid for morning tea with a Wedgwood service of 1820 and French cutlery of the nineteenth century. The small chair that is visible is a very rare nineteenth-century Austrian piece that includes a musical box that plays a waltz when one sits down on it. Claudio Zanettin, who is responsible for the entire interior design of the home, collected the art objects and antiques.

Left: Here we are in the gentle countryside of Umbria, in a splendid dwelling where the illusionist furnishings produce a marble effect and the brightly-painted walls echo the variegated and dominant greens, deep browns and generally rich tonalities of the surrounding nature. In the dining room, a round nineteenth-century table, placed opposite the walnut bread cupboard, is ready for the morning coffee, served in a very fine *bone china service*. Local earthenware and *barbotines are hung over the dresser.*

Below left: The enchanted garden of Villa Gamberaia in Settignano, much praised by D'Annunzio, who loved to stroll among its "baroque arrangements of scenes," water terraces and shrubbery masterfully sculpted in accordance with the most rigorous dictates of the *ars topiaria,* so appreciated by Edith Wharton, create a sumptuous setting for the table laid for breakfast with dainty golden cups by Versace Rosenthal. Two tiny portions of Sacher torte on dessert plates accompany the aromatic beverage.

Below right: In this Florence garden coffee is served with small crisp short pastry biscuits, in valuable cups designed by Versace for Rosenthal.

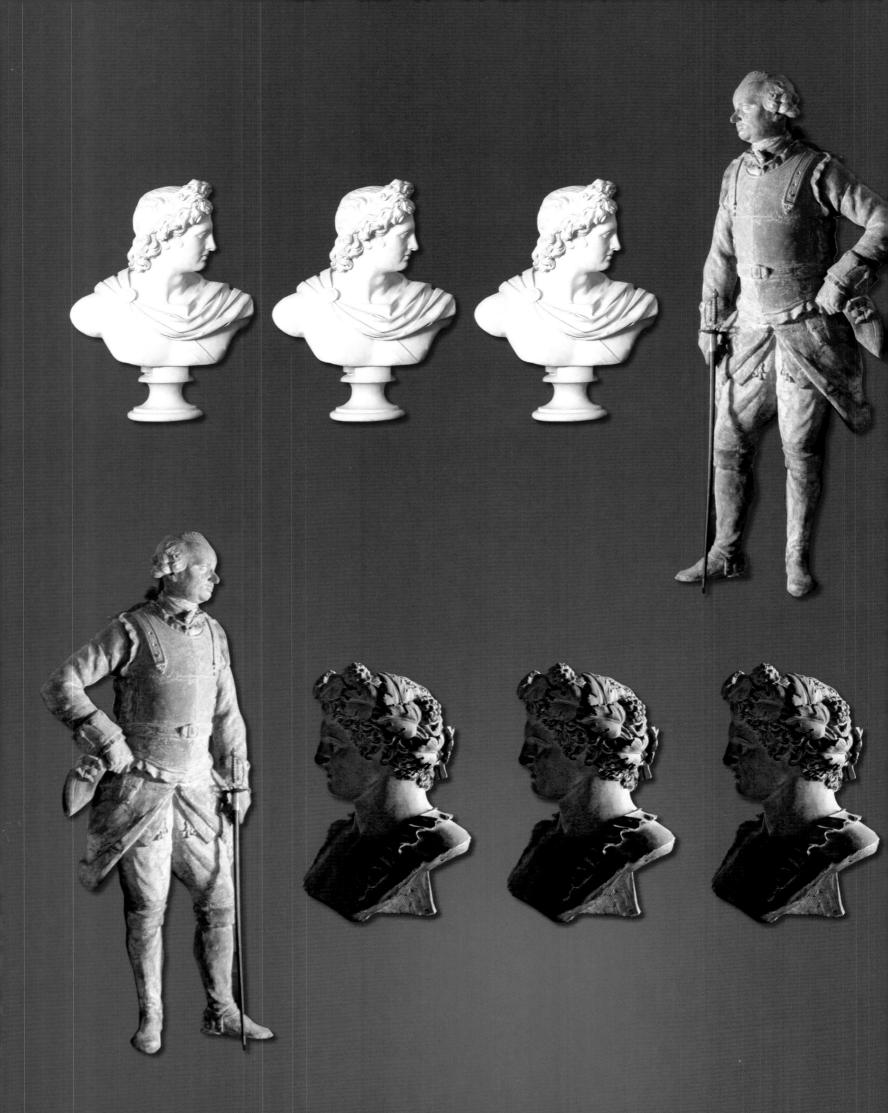

With an Artist's Eye

The intent gaze of ancestors who stare from pictures hung on the walls. The blind sockets of ancient busts. Pictures, frescoes, stuccowork, entire porcelain services hung on the walls.... How does the laid table fit in with an intensely artistic *milieu*?

Magnificently, needless to say. The stable and ephemeral elements mirror one another, confront one another and engage in a dialogue of forms and colours.

The Gothic revival chairs and roses reminiscent of *Biedermeier* are in tune with the quiet romanticism of a nineteenth-century picture gallery. The terseness of the tempera landscapes with ruins on the wall culminates in a triumph of whiteness in the central laid table.

A crowded baroque atmosphere imposes eighteenth-century porcelains; the bold exotic colours of a drawing room à la Matisse welcome the Chinese note of a tea ceremony. The severity of Art Deco and metaphysical painting inspire tables that are rigorously geometric, even minimalist.

Above, right: The dining room is important for receiving guests in the house/study of a Brescia professional, part of a magnificent Empire style palazzo. Here the table is laid in a decidedly formal way below the stately ceiling, surely frescoed after the unification of Italy, depicting four children in different poses that symbolically represent the fledgling country. Intense blues dominate the room, including the *surrizzo* velvet used to dress up the table and to cover the upholstered chairs with lacquer and gold frame.

White and blue are the colours of the Chinese, Japanese and European porcelains that form a collection gathered at the end of the room in front of a large painting by Carle van Loo (1705-1765) portraying King of France Louis XV with three of his favourites.

Following pages: just outside Rome a stately villa built by Andrea Busiri Vici offers the occasion to take a leap into the past. Rather than villa, it might be better described as a combination house and library or house and museum owing to the rare books, art objects, paintings, sculptures and marbles of the classic and Renaissance period conserved there. In a tidy little room, the dinner table is arranged in front of a large sixteenth-century Venetian canvas with mythological subject matter.

Above: Arched apertures and ribbed ceiling transform the dining room of this original sixteenth-century Milan home into a sort of open gallery. As in the rest of the house, the walls deliberately left with peeling plaster feature trompe-l'œil paintings with subject matter suggesting archaeological recoveries, dreamy metaphysical landscapes with traces of Lombardy.

The late eighteenth-century walnut dinner table has chairs from Lombardy of the same period; overhead is a rare nineteenth-century bronze Russian chandelier. The portrait *Homage to Vouet* is the work of a young Spanish painter, a pupil of Lila de Nobili.

Left: The dining room of this Marches villa, all painted in the illusionist style like a prodigious funhouse mirror by nineteenth-century master Egidio Coppola, is frescoed in the manner of an exotic Art Nouveau conservatory, verdant with palms, ivy and vine shoots, trees and shrubs. The floor has a chequered pattern, as is customary in greenhouses, orangeries and winter gardens.

The table is laid with an antique porcelain service by Copeland.

Following pages: East and West, baroque and neo-classic furnishings, and decorations inspired by Turkish and Indian *mezzeri* meet in the dining room of a Milan palazzo built – a rare event for the city – on Roman foundations. Here the table, illuminated by gilded bronze candelabra and a Moroccan light fixture, is covered with a runner and even the walls are painted, directly on the rough plaster, with patterns drawn from the Middle Eastern world or courts of the maharajahs.

Above, right: Rare collections of paintings, sculptures and art objects enliven the rooms of this historical Paris dwelling in Saint-Germain-des-Pres, adjoining the atelier of Delacroix. The house is a mix of family home, labyrinth, artist's studio, castle and *cabinet de curiosité; its rooms defy* traditional classification and follow one another without definite functions, renewing an ancient architectural custom abandoned in the nineteenth century: according to the mood of the master of the house or number of guests, from time to time any space can be turned into a drawing room or library, while here and there the table can be laid with porcelain, crystal and silver – in the French style, as Madame Bonnivet, Stendhal's famous creation, would have done, perhaps, as on this occasion, by the statue of Charles Ledesme of Saint-Elix.

Following pages, left: One dines with art in the Tuscany villa of Roberto Cavalli, built around a medieval tower. The table, laid under a large nineteenth-century Symbolist painting, features a red dévorée silk tablecloth by Cavalli and a pair of sixteenth-century gilded bronze flasks; it accurately reflects the inventive, incessantly changing world of the stylist and his daring, opulent, telluric, scintillating life. All the ingredients are there: Renaissance inspiration, unbridled and blazing colouring….

Following pages, right: In Lunigiana, among ruins, forbidding towers and iron-grey castles, rosy Villa Malaspina is a brilliant example of a harmonious balance of eras and styles. Here, where the *spino fiorito* (thorn in bloom) branch of the Malaspina family – the other branch being referred to as *spino secco or withered thorn* – loved to enjoy the holidays in peace and quiet, far from the burdens of leadership and political and military strategies, the table is laid in the dining room before a fireplace framed by Carrara marble with volutes and a trompe-l'œil that seems to lend continuity to a series of communicating rooms.

Preceding pages: Crystal by Sévres, exquisite porcelains, lace tablecloth and solid silver candelabra enhance dining in the gallery on Gothic Revival chairs à la Pugin, surrounded by walls painted Pompeii red and adorned by a rich picture gallery with eighteenth- and nineteenth-century works, under the benevolent gaze of forebears in austere poses mingled with peaceful examples of landscape painting.

Above left: At the restaurant of the Hotel Astoria in St Petersburg, a city of metaphysical beauty created in 1703 from the dreams and fantasies of Peter the Great, one dines under the portrait of the czar, on porcelain plates by Lomonosov, at one time the manufactory of the Romanovs.

Above right: In the Paris residence of prominent Italian theatre personalities Ezio Frigerio and Franca Squarciapino, the cultivated and eccentric magnificence of the French aristocracy of the ancien régime lives on beside Italian luxuries. The sixteenth-century Italian walnut dinner table is laid with a nineteenth-century Hungarian porcelain service. The large Italian painting dates from the eighteenth century; the rare tapestry of silk and linen is French.

Right: Miami's "Casa Casuarina," built by eccentric architect, philanthropist and heir to the Standard Oil fortune Alden Freeman, was the *buen retiro* of Gianni Versace and now has been turned into an exclusive private club. Unique and scintillating, it is the setting for important worldly events.
The dining room has mosaic pebble walls designed by Gianni Versace; the tables are laid with plates by Versace Rosenthal.

Above: Dinner in the kitchen of the home of a Florence antique dealer. Square white porcelain plates grace a maple table by the cooking unit of *botticino* marble. The 1932 oil, *Portrait of Myrtia Ciarlantini, is by* Giovanni Guerrini.

Right: The rarefied, minimal atmosphere of this Bologna dining room is underscored by Gregorio Cuartas' metaphysical painting hung on the rear wall, the suggestive *Ferruccio* iron chairs by Roberto Mora and the squared silver leaf console by Dilmos. The now famous steel and ground glass table *Il Doge* by Carlo Scarpa is laid with straw place mats, enamelled bowls and glass plates by Bormioli.

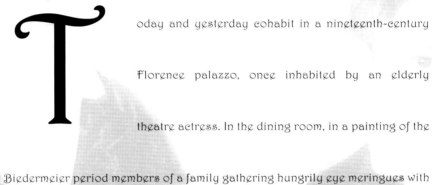

Today and yesterday cohabit in a nineteenth-century Florence palazzo, once inhabited by an elderly theatre actress. In the dining room, in a painting of the Biedermeier period members of a family gathering hungrily eye meringues with whipped cream on porcelain stands.

The silver heron with ostrich egg, resting on a late nineteenth-century Tuscany walnut console, is of Germanic origin and is dated 1850.

Above: French-style table setting in a Paris home includes porcelain plates placed directly on the nineteenth-century mahogany table. On the wall, a suggestive "mosaic" of gouaches, sketches and whimsical architectural elements.

Right: In Riad, under a large surrealistic painting, we have a table laid in the European style with porcelains and crystal to confirm the geographical *déplacement* of the scene. The modern and vaguely ethnic note is provided by the very fine linen runners, used in place of tablecloth or American-style place mats.

Hints of nostalgia, dramatic contrasts, explosions of exuberant Mediterranean colours enliven these Paris interiors, leading the owner, born in Algeria, on the road to dreamland. The Moroccan-style tea is served in the living room before a small early twentieth-century Chinese divan and a piece of Louis Quinze furniture; the 1937 portrait of a woman above the divan is by Stanislas Floch.

Ancient Dwellings

Only the spacious elaborate layouts of old palazzi and villas, where the dining room is connected with other receiving rooms, service areas and arcades, are able to confer on laid tables a historical charm such as to take us back in time. Under such circumstances, between one chair and the next, we almost expect to see the court paintings of the eighteenth century come to life, with bewigged servants in livery forming a circle around the aristocratic tables.

Revisited in our day, the long tables able to seat twenty or more guests maintain their serial nature, inducing the photographer to frame them with giddy perspective effects: narrowing rows of chair backs, rosaries of plates and forests of glasses. Here more than elsewhere the centrepiece (or centrepieces) is called on to hold our gaze lest it lose itself in the obsessive and egalitarian repetition of chairs and tableware.

The unique piece of artistic workmanship, placed directly under the chandelier, works wonderfully as a sort of landmark indicating the midpoint of the table: a group of silver or bisque statues or a miniature fountain are worthy heirs to the triumphal pomp that gladdened the tables of the powerful in the baroque age. No less effective is the punctuation of the centre line with symmetrical sequences of various objects – vases, candelabra and salt cellars – to break the monotony.

Here and only here can an ostentatious sideboard be included naturally or a service of valuable dinnerware be arranged for purely decorative purposes and – as in former times – a show of magnificence. Holdovers of noble habits progressively become bourgeois in *fin de siècle drawing rooms*, where the *étagère was put to such uses, today evoking remote lifestyles whose stamp is conserved within the confines of the walls* that witnessed them.

Above: The Madrid residence of the von Thyssen-Bornemisza family, owners of one of the world's major art collections, teems with suggestions of the Orient. The exotic family spirit, tempered by a strictly Central European upbringing – the Thyssens were among the leading steel makers in the Germany of Kaiser Wilhelm II – can be found in the table setting after the classical style.

The lovely nineteenth-century mahogany table, surrounded by coeval chairs and lit by a Bohemian crystal chandelier, is set with German porcelain plates decorated with floral motifs of Oriental inspiration, while the crystal goblets are engraved with grapevines, symbol of fertility and the joie de vivre so much a part of popular culture in Bavaria and the Rhineland.

Right: Lord Harold Acton, "prince" of the Anglo-Florentines and one of the supreme masters of Liberalism, lived here his entire life. We are at Villa La Pietra, a magnificent example of Renaissance architecture in the Florence area. "At times," he once said, "I feel like nothing more than a custodian, but I was born here and, like Candide, I think that each of us ought to cultivate his own garden. And I consider myself fortunate to have this garden to tend; I am aware that I am privileged and that I belong to a bygone age."

The gilded solitude of Acton is well represented by this "frugal" but refined place setting for one that seems a leaf out of a history book: exquisite crystal and silver before a Renaissance fireplace with carved while marble moulding and surrounded by masterpieces of religious art.

At *Palazzo Durazzo Pallavicini* – built in Genoa by architect Bianco in the seventeenth century and thoroughly reworked by Tagliafieni in the eighteenth century – dining is done in a room with walls decorated with grotesques, a frescoed *trompe-l'œil* ceiling and the sparkling light of a flamboyant crystal chandelier.

The neo-classic *milieu*, with a few nineteenth-century touches, makes for a measured table setting, refreshed by the naturalistic decor of the porcelain service and flowery centrepiece.

We might be at the court of the czars or King of Prussia or some Renaissance prince. Everything has the glint of gold and silver on this table photographed in Los Angeles: the cutlery with engraved handles, the plates with elaborate edges, the goblets, the glasses and the sumptuous centrepiece placed on a green marble top. This splendid table setting is part of the sensational decorative and applied arts objects of the estate of Arthur and Rosalinde Gilbert, willed to the foundation bearing their name.

Below, right: As in the Age of Enlightenment when the passion for *chinoiserie exploded,* this splendid ebony table is laid with silver and faceted shining crystal, beside a Chinese screen painted with scenes of everyday life at the imperial court. Furthermore, every place setting resembles a Flemish still life where the white lace, dazzling precious metals and the shapes of the bread loaves play fundamental roles.

Following pages: A page of history: the time is now but the scene recalls the sumptuous stylistic eclecticism of late nineteenth-century aristocratic dwellings as described by Fogazzaro and D'Annunzio, where fabulous medieval and nineteenth-century pieces intermingled. The sixteenth-century Italian table is laid with flowery nineteenth-century Hungarian porcelain. Watching over the table is a hieratic Virgin with Babe and Saints of the Siena school, surrounded by two polychrome stuccoes of a few centuries later and a Madonna and Child after della Robbia.

Above: Elegant dinner in a Florence palazzo. The tablecloth is of embroidered linen, while the goblets, cups and flutes of clear and ruby crystal are edged with first-quality gold, as are the bone china plates. Cutlery and ewer are silver. A low centrepiece composed of white calla lilies in a silver bowl discreetly catches the eye of table companions without obstructing their view.

Left: "It is a fine specimen of the modern buildings of Madrid, which are giving the city the sumptuous look of a great city." This verdict appeared in a 1917 issue of *Architettura e Costruzione* on the building that in 1936 would become the home of the Italian Embassy in Madrid. In designing it, architect Joaquín Rojí drew heavily on his conception of French baroque, so much so that it seemed like the residence of a much earlier era.

Here we are in a hall used for receptions; the restrained elegance of the table suggests settings of the seventeenth and eighteenth centuries. The row of plates and chairs lends a sense of order, while the silver centrepiece and Murano chandelier communicate a sentiment of cultivated refinement.

Right: Los Angeles is the location of Villa Los Tiempos, a sumptuous piece of pure beaux-arts architecture, once the unofficial outpost of the White House on the West Coast. Presidents Eisenhower, Kennedy, Johnson and Nixon all stayed there.

Today it is home to an important collector and keen "hunter" – among other things – of neo-classic obelisks. Here one dines with great formal elegance on a long mahogany table able to accommodate over twenty guests; it is laid with a porcelain and gold leaf service designed by Elsa Peretti for Tiffany.

Following pages: Where are Antonine Carême and Anthelme Brillat-Savarin? The barely sketched setting of this table echoes the gastronomic architectures of the former and the decorative logic of the latter to bear comparison with the gilded magnificence *à la française* of the setting, mindful of the *boudoirs* of Madame Pompadour or the bountiful salons where Charles-Maurice Talleyrand orchestrated his cynical and sumptuous "fork diplomacy."

Colours at Table and Surroundings

Anyone who lays table amid bold colours, even including the table linen and dinnerware, shows brave confidence in the aesthetic value of his (or her) cuisine because vivid solid colours, pure shades and daring combinations are enemies of food or at least compete visually with it. A minestrone with its different vegetables, *pappa al pomodoro*, greyish tripe salad, browned meatloaf or dark stew made with game do not go with brilliant colours, instead calling for more agreeable natural burnt earth tones. Bright colours do agree with dairy products, tomatoes, peppers, salmon, black and pink caviar, sliced kiwi, strawberries and melons, all part of a dazzling and varied gastronomic palette. Also pleasing are the geometric creations of Japanese sushi and other dishes of Oriental cuisine, based on neat shapes and sharp contrasts.

The energy emanating from rich, bold colours, perhaps combined with stripes and floral patterns, certainly makes the meal an experience bordering on contemporary art, which is the interpreter par excellence of colour. Chromatic extremes touch on the walls, upholstery and the very table.

And at the extremity of decorative taste with a nod to *horror vacui* we may chance to find on a tablecloth imitating green malachite – one of the most brazen stones found in nature, in tone with the painted finishing touches of the glass door – bright golden service plates with bowls decorated with fleshy lotus flowers and holding unfamiliar soups, with the centre of the table occupied by a composite trophy of madrepores, mother-of-pearl, salt crystals and gilded metal animals, in the middle of a bedlam of *naturalia* and *artificialia* that makes the whole room a very up-to-date *Wunderkammer* with a whiff of the Orient.

Preceding pages: Mixing the sacred and the profane, at the Hotel Tugu of Bali one dines in the temple. The dining room of the resort is in fact an authentic Bale Sutra or Pavilion of Harmony, an eighteenth-century Kang Xi Chinese temple, transported and reassembled here piece by piece, devoted to Balinese heroes and symbol of the harmony of Balinese and Chinese culture. The menu offers Peranakan cuisine or Chinese and Indonesian, served with Western-style tableware, with a few colourful exotic concessions.

Above: Decorated with verve and irony by playful designer Carlo Rampazzi, a villa in the Belgian countryside is brightened by brushstrokes of colour and furnishings with unusual and provocative lines. The dining room table of the "Costantino" collection by Rampazzi has a tooled leather top and oxidised bronze legs. The centrepiece is a Flemish-style "still life" of fruit and vegetables.

Left: Plaster walls with bold colours and panels made with multicoloured fabrics personalise this Turin interior. Here every room has been given a Latin name; the dining room, *Locus Studii,* is dominated by green walls and a huge textile wall hanging. The nearby walnut table dating from the early the twentieth century is extendable; edged in gold, it is laid with a Bavarian porcelain service.

Preceding pages: Marked by dazzling inventive eccentricity, the Beverly Hills residence of major decorator Tony Duquette features decidedly bright, eclectic rooms. The dining room, carved out of what was once a garage, recalls a garden if not a *Wunderkammer*.

The table display includes old Chinese bowls complete with cover, Venetian glass, imitation coral and rock crystal.

The Chinese cabinet houses collections of jewellery designed by Duquette and partner Tony Wilkinson.

Above, right: An apartment in an eighteenth-century Chiasso palazzo is a journey through the centuries, defined by colour: vivid walls, varnished and enamelled furnishings, gaudy fabrics. The dining room ceiling has green and blue vaults frescoed with a view of Manhattan; an eighteenth-century pendulum clock is covered with blue and gold damask. The table, dating from the 1930s, is laid with ceramic plates from the 1950s and Murano glasses.

We are in Forte dei Marmi, a city in Versilia that becomes an art capital in the summertime. In this house candles provide the lighting and old Moroccan decorations and softly draped Indian fabrics bespeak the Oriental seduction of outdoor life. The tea ritual takes place in the kitchen, seated on nineteenth-century Chinese bamboo chairs.

Above: The Orient viewed from the West. In the dining room of this house in Verona's San Fermo district, where everything speaks of bygone times, exotic styles mingle with modern lines of design. The *wengé* table is laid with Chinese porcelain plates; a picture in the background, inspired by the detail of a Chinese door, includes gold writing.

Right: A table setting at the Saffron Restaurant of the Banyan Tree Hotel in the unspoiled paradise of the Seychelles. The mahogany table is laid with a few ethnic details in line with the dictates of the fusion style. The chair is mellowed by showy silk cushions.

Above: Often it is the details that determine the aesthetic quality of a scene. In this Milan dining room a slender narwhal tusk against a red panel background creates an impression of order and symmetry that adds depth and mystical suggestion to the minimalist setting.

Left: In Brescia, on Borgo Wüehrer where a brewery of the same name was located, at the foot of Maddalena hill, a loft of over 200 square metres with a vast terrace appears to float above the city. Here in the dining room cultivated eclecticism is the watchword with classic hints underlining the bond with tradition, such the gold leaf chairs that take up the tonality of the walls.

A few ethnic touches include tea glasses from Morocco, while much modern design is evident in the *Saggina* light fixture by Minital Lux, *wengé* table and vase by Venini in the middle of the table. The works on the wall are by David Tremlet.

Below left: In a Miami apartment the clear brilliance of contemporary furnishings gathers and expands the airy luminosity of the urban landscape. The breakfast nook in the kitchen is defined by the milky white of the *Panton Chairs* designed by Verner Panton for Vitra, which accompany the enamelled doors of the cupboards.

Lower right: Oriental suggestions and Mediterranean spirit in this eighteenth-century palazzo overlooking the Canal Grande, where Diego Dalla Palma has found "the pleasure of a picture postcard *Serenissima* together with the more variegated one of the Venice of mystery." In this *buen retiro* and bright observatory sheltered from the tourist clamour, Dalla Palma experiences "that vibrant silence that it is possible to savour only in Venice." In the dining room, plays of transparencies are produced by glasses, plates and table, all of glass and designed by the genial image creator.

Right: White, including that of the lights, is the dominant colour in the rarefied spatial composition of a Paris interior in a lovely building from the Haussmann era, inhabited by interior designer Florence Pucci.
The pieces of grey enamel and steel furniture in the kitchen and the dining area were conceived by the designer, who favours the conceptual unity of rooms, furnishings and colour. The *Vaisseau "céleste"* light fixture is a luminous sculpture by Daniel Baumann. Chairs by Verner Panton for Vitra are drawn up to the white table brightened by touches of red.

Above: Rigor in black and white: only the food is red, like a brushstroke by Mondrian, in a Paris interior where everything is marked by design. A black polypropylene chair is pulled up to a white resin table where black ceramic service dishes, flat white plates and black soup plates alternate.

Left: Designed with elegant simplicity, the Cortina residence of Anna Fendi joins early twentieth-century Austrian furnishings, contemporary art works and objects crafted by local artisans. "Something that has always fascinated me," the stylist explains, "is the rigor, the orderliness that Cortina manages to impose on anyone who goes there: here elegance is always measured and restrained."
In Cortina, Anna Fendi loves to lay the old majolica kitchen table with local glass and ceramics: "I like to maintain the original character of the houses where I live, but also to seek and find objects, transforming and recombining them.
I never follow a trend or current taste; in any home of mine there is always an assembly of moods. Different objects and furnishings amalgamate, stratify and overlap naturally."

A mingling of styles, but with a sense of measure and great elegance, in an attic just outside Brescia.

Here the dining area, like the rest of the house, is dominated by the contrast between the ivory tone of the walls and dark brown of the sliding doors and *wengé* moulding around the ceiling. The optical work over the fireplace is signed by Viselli.

The piece of Tibetan furniture dates from the eighteenth century. The white table with the oak top is by Studio Linea; on it rest plates with huge red roses by Mikasa, Murano drinking glasses and a Flemish candelabrum.

The huge chandelier is Murano glass; the Italian sword on the wall dates from the nineteenth century.

Above: In Ekensberg, in the eighteenth-century Swedish residence of art historian Lars Sjoeberg, faithfully restored, all the charm of the Gustav III style re-emerges. The dining room, with the characteristic rough parquet, is dominated by the typical majolica stove. The eye-catching bust before the window is a likeness of Lady Hamilton.

The table, surrounded by small Gustav III chairs, displays a simple setting that tends to deny the difference between host and guests, and to exalt the wholly Scandinavian concept of friendship without distinction of origin or wealth.

Right: Bright plays of colour describe the discreet elegance of a Rome interior, where precious objects delight the eye with the seductive aura of bygone days. Gothic revival candlesticks rest on the Louis Seize table, along with a four-tier fruitstand holding mushrooms and vegetables, porcelains, fishes, eggs and bread loaves reminiscent of a Flemish still life. On the shelves of the sideboard is a rare service of the Indies Company. The Louis Seize wall lamps are wood.

Above: As though touched by King Midas, a small Paris mansard, redesigned by imaginative owner Carlo Rampazzi, shines with gold and celestial lights. The droplights of the mansard are gilded, while the powerful trusses of the roof are silvered; the kitchen and tiny dining area float amid the clouds of a sky painted an unexpected colour, a trompe-l'œil by Sergio Villa.
The Louis Quinze table is laid with a French porcelain service, coloured crystal, and a crystal and brass Napoleon III sweet holder, which excellently interpret the fairy-tale sentiment of the setting.

Right: Decidedly daring chromatic and stylistic contrasts characterise this apartment overlooking the church of Saint-Sulpice, in a seventeenth-century Paris mansion. The kitchen is furnished in rustic style: a nineteenth-century table is used for dining as well as a worktable, while the dresser holds vases, Renaissance engravings, a collection of antique glasses and small objects and toys.
The painting on the wall is by Fernand Labat.

Lower left: Ethnic and vaguely gypsy hints emanate from this table adorned with drapes and colours suggestive of the Orient, illuminated by transparent glass, long tapers and small candleholders. Curtains and fabrics are arranged all around to make the scene more intimate, almost as though alluding to the volutes of the small spiral stone column.

*Lower right: The seaside Pa*lm Beach residence of an American art collector filters classic architecture through a contemporary sensibility. The Irish table in the dining area is laid with a naturalistic spirit, displaying seashell decorations and speckled boxes. A painting by Patrick Dumbar graces the wall.

Left: In the living room of a Turin apartment the red, yellow, blue and green tones symbolise the four seasons. The chairs, which take up the red of the wall, are covered with French damask, while red, blue, yellow and green crystal goblets rest on the long table. The hung panel is covered with different fabrics.

The Collector's Table

With collections in the dining room, living together is intense, close, almost hand-to-hand. Each day and at every meal the huge stag antlers jut out from the wall, the mirrors reflect a myriad of images, the light gleams exactly the same on the shiny surfaces of the porcelains, and the amphorae forever stand out against the light wall with their graceful handles and pronounced mouths.

The presence of similar allied objects impends, conditions and commands over all the rest, suggesting correspondences and inspiring choices of materials. A set of majestic celadon green vases may have guided the decision to cover the chairs with a similar colour.

A collection of Palissy trays or *palissystes* swarming with reptiles, fishes and shellfish act as a stimulus to serve lobsters and shrimps adventurously on plates in the shape of *Pecten jacobaeus*, half a dozen per plate.

Geometric panelling in the Art Deco manner with silvery and golden tints goes well with a black and white table with metal goblets and glasses.

These pages: Antonio Coppola is a *sui generis* designer and collector. He loves to collect almost anything, giving free rein to his eclectic temperament. Rather than putting the objects in order, he juxtaposes them to create relaxing and fanciful atmospheres.

And so it happens that objects of the most varied inspiration have accumulated on and around this table, including Picasso ceramics, finely crafted *tajine* and designer light fixtures, all joined aesthetically by a sunny taste in colours.

Preceding pages: The Al Maha Desert Resort is a 5-star dream place a few miles from Dubai. In addition to being the flagship of international hoteldom, it is a small-scale museum of Arab and Bedouin culture. This feature is noticeable in every suite, just as in the lobby. Everywhere illuminated wall niches, almost like showcases, display valuable polished copper utensils. The same is true of the tables where swan-beak teapots pour refreshing green tea. A world that might have been invented by Aladdin....

A table made to order for a tête-à-tête, in a truly unusual setting that seems borrowed from a crude anatomic painting by Damien Hirsch more than a trompe-l'œil. We are in a twentieth-century farmstead on the "della Mandria" estate near Turin. Architect Paolo Genta Ternavasio composed the interior design by drawing inspiration from the decorative world of Pauline de Rothschild. In his words, this required "Balancing great richness with *understatement* in view of creating a fairly rustic ambient, where nonetheless disorienting objects might materialise."

Above: The force of contrast. On the wall, the dynamism of futurist works "caged" by orderly pilasters; on the table, an austere Oriental-style setting: the energy of opposites gives rise to a suggestive atmosphere reminiscent of theatre.

Left: Here, according to Alain Resnais, is the home of Revolution: simplicity and incisive signs, a brand of collecting that smacks of symbolism. Two hunting trophies hung on cream walls keep watch over a frugal supper, typical of *citoyens*. It is the Paris of image that transforms the almost rough simplicity into a matter of luxury.

A perfect twentieth-century style setting frames this French table with mirror top crowded with collector's items: a 1920s vase with scorpion by Ferruccio Mengaroni and, above all, plates by Manifattura Galvani decorated with a stylised sailboat motif typical of Italian graphic work of the early 1930s.
The Murano glass ceiling lamp dating from the 1930s is by Venini, while a 1940 De Ruta vase on the dresser depicts a bullfight.

Above: Here the table seems to be a complement: stealing the show is the seventeenth-century painting that, with its dazzling gilt frame, crowns the fireplace and, above all, the collection of plates hung everywhere on the walls with an order so well-calculated and cogent as to appear almost informal.

Left: The dining nook of a Cortina home. The wood that elegantly lines the walls and ceiling, together with a painted rural scene and collection of keepsakes, communicates a sense of warm intimacy. The table is dressed up with a locally-produced tablecloth luxuriant with floral and geometric patterns, contributing to the atmosphere with a breakfast setting of Ladin inspiration: plates and cups decorated with local flowers, teapot with two spouts, cutlery with bone handles and traditional loaves of bread.

Following pages: Living room and dining area interpenetrate in an unusual way in this *hôtel particulier* of Paris. There is practically no break between divan and table; the green of the one seems to spring from the floral centrepiece and small blue armchairs that surround the other. The collection of large mirrors adorning the walls contributes to this chromatic/symbiotic effect.

Above: Like a magic box, a tiny flat in the heart of Cortina becomes an ingenious container of surprises and suggestions. Woodwork that dissimulates equipped walls and sliding panels, details that draw attention away from other parts of the house, plays of equilibrium and well thought out choices of furnishings and objects produced the miracle, illusionistically expanding the space and making it intimate and comfortable. In the dining area, separated from the kitchen by a sixteenth-century Venetian glass door that acts as a service hatch, the table is flanked on three sides by a bench, like in a *stube*, and lit by a sculptural wood light fixture with deer antlers from the nineteenth century. A seventeenth-century Venetian angel stands on the windowsill.

Left: On the traces of Thackeray from London to the Orient: the theme of the setting whose eclectic inspiration finds a common denominator in the celadon green framing the large round table.

Green is found in the cushions of the Indian nickel silver chairs, Chinese vases, porcelain plates and napkins.

The roses composing the centrepiece bouquet recall the romantic glory of the English countryside.

Below, right: In his own way, the gourmet is a collector who gathers and savours flavours and gustatory emotions. In this case, the pleasure of the beauty expressed in the masterpieces of decorative art ringing the table laid with crystal and silver is associated with the delights of the palate: marvellous Renaissance plates with mythological motifs, small seventeenth-century architectural whims and countless other objects of charm beyond words. The setting, a sixteenth-century Siena villa reworked by architect Maurizio Chiari, contributes no little to the aesthetic triumph.

Following pages: In Trouville, a pavilion for balls of the Second Empire has been transformed into a cosy home for receiving friends. The available space was turned to good use by installing a loft for the bedrooms; below, a dining nook has been carved out that also acts as a library. The ceramic plates by Bernard Palissay collected on the wall have motifs based on the marine world, as do those used to lay the table. Small black leather Louis Seize style armchairs ring the nineteenth-century table.

Left: Everything is ready in the winter garden of a Rome residence for laying the table with the luxury of a bygone age. An early nineteenth-century cast iron candelabrum rests on a pile of porcelain plates. The two tall cachepots from the same period are also cast iron. Instead, the crystal candelabrum dates from the eighteenth century. The Empire tray has a mirror base and gilded bronze edge. To the rear a Louis Philippe cage, nineteenth-century candelabrum and 1940 lamp rest on the kitchen table dating from the late eighteenth century.

Following pages, left: Dreamlike gears and fantastic furnishings populate the Milan home of Paola and Roberto Fallani, Florence artists and designers. In front of a screen with glazed panels decorated by Angelo Rinaldi with ardour reminiscent of Depero, the glass tabletop seems suspended as if by magnetic levitation. The white plates and large black service plates, silver goblets and glasses by Brandimarte, bronze Persian candleholder by Igor Mitoraj, and iron and glass lamp by Fallani confer the scene with a sentiment joining poetic energy and an incisive constructivist touch.

Following pages, right: In the home of designer and horror film actress Anouska Hempel, the common living space is marked by a mélange of ethnic, Art Deco and neo-classic styles. As though conjured up by subterranean forces, a sort of table of mystery springs from this aesthetic mix: black, in keeping with the contemporary trend, apparently casual in its decoration where small lamps engage in dialogue with columns crowned with miniature urns, encircled by equally black chairs and with a bizarre overhead light fixture in the shape of bells turned upside down, is harks back to initiation ceremonies *à la* Christina of Sweden. The silvery plates and white napkins complete the esoteric dimension.

EXOTIC TABLES

Beginning from the nineteenth century, Europe experienced waves of passion for the Orient in its every visual expression, to the extent of leading to a flowering of Orientalism of every kind in the arts, literature and music. Even though today travel to many Asian countries is no longer an adventure reserved for just a few but a dream within the reach of many, exotic tables have lost none of their allure. The possibilities include lacquers, bronzes, porcelains, panels and exquisitely ornate screens, in addition to smooth woods, earthenware and plain plaited fibres.

These are the languages of the Orient: variegated and composite, the same as always but open to endless variations. Indeed, the art and furnishings of Oriental civilisations being timeless in the age-old continuity of shapes, materials and colours, the ancient and contemporary meet and get confused when viewed with our inexpert Western eyes.

All it takes is the silhouette of a palm against the fading twilight and blue of an ocean to provide any table with an ambience of intense charm.

The colours and motifs of the mighty untamed nature of Africa instead inform other tables: spotted and striped fabrics, and earthy and burnt tones make every dinner an imaginary safari.

Preceding pages: Dominating the dining room of an old Florence home is a large screen with four sections resembling a glass door. The birds in flight above a foaming sea were executed by Galileo Chini, inspired by the art of Siam.

The table setting takes up the Orientalised tone and colour scheme with place green mats with lotus flowers and small plates of a red lacquer colour.

This page: A few steps from Santa Maria Novella in Florence, Giancarlo Antognoni – unforgettable member of Italy's world champion football team in 1982 – has opened a restaurant with an exotic air called the Kilimangiaro Cafè, where the focus is on ethnic cuisine. Special dishes include shark soup flavoured with coconut and pork in pineapple sauce.

One of the dining rooms features a South African light fixture adorned with kudo horns and ostrich eggs. The *privé*, designed by Lorenzo Gemma, has upholstered *animalier* wall panelling, while the table is hand-decorated by Paola Poggiolini. Architect Roberto Morlacci designed the benches, chairs and cushions.

Following pages: It is a time of ascetic minimalism: we are in Bagan's Nat Taung kyaung monastery in Myanmar. Today the eighteenth-century building is home to about ten monks. Here the passing hours, days and years are marked only by the sound of the hammer striking a huge piece of hollow bamboo placed at the entrance of the building. It calls the monks to prayer and the offering of simple meals served in the typical black lacquer bowl.

Preceding pages: The scene resembles a painting by René Magritte or Edward Hopper: it is metaphysical, surrealist, or so realistic as to become unreal. We are on the beach of the Altamer Resort in Shoal Bay West on the island of Anguilla in the Caribbean; the table between two seaside armchairs is soberly laid for a breakfast that has the flavour of a dream. The colours of the fruit enliven the table, while nature – the sand, palms and wavy sea forming the backdrop – "invents" the dining room.

Right: There are no panes in the windows of "Racheta Cavallona" in Los Samanes in the Dominican Republic: the sun and musical silence of the tropical forest flow, enlivening the space with subtle romantic hints. The palm wood lining the dining room walls gives it a pinkish cast. The white chairs and the table with its plant motif stand were fashioned by skilled local craftsmen.
The table is laid to match the surrounding pastels.

Following pages: An intimate dining area has been created in the light and shade of the lofts of the African residence of Flavio Briatore, which recalls certain dwellings of consuls and merchants immortalised in black and white photographs of the late nineteenth century at the time when the Black Continent was being explored. "Here," says Briatore, "what I am seeking above all is freedom. Kenya has a generous, hospitable soul. It is my refuge far from the tiresome stage of appearances."

Above: Themes of local tradition and European inspiration intermingle on the dining room table of a Bangkok apartment. The decorative thrust is entrusted to a refined hand-painted *Thai* porcelain service but the aesthetic fulcrum of the table setting is the gay centrepiece of vivid flowers not yet open.

*Left: The calm, friendly h*ospitality of Bali pervades this table of the Hotel Tugu situated on the slopes of the Agung volcano. The buffet-style breakfast on straw mats and bamboo offers a wide variety of exotic fruit amid colours and fragrances that inebriate the senses.

Above: At Great House, on the island of Barbados, dinner for two is served on a simple wood platform in direct contact with the beach. The Versace Home Collection plates made by Rosenthal colour the table in keeping with the dreamy atmosphere of the time and place.

Right: At night, candlelight adds to the unforgettable exotic charm of the terrace of the Sandoway Resort in Myanmar. The rattan armchairs are produced in Yangong; the lamps have been fashioned from galvanised sheet. The plates are the typical work of Burmese craftsmen, left rough before finishing with lacquer.

Preceding pages: This table, laid on the Balinese beach of Cangi renowned for its fiery sunsets, echoes the tints of the sky. The floral composition amid the plates, typical of the culture of Bali, is called Janur and is formed by petals arranged on palm leaves, while the presentation of the silver platter follows the laying of the table used for "imperial Chinese" dinners where recipes from the Ming and Ching dynasties are combined.

Above: Dinner for two in the Saudi desert: an experience so thrilling as to make everything else, beginning from the table, a "minor" matter. And yet, it is an indispensable element. Everything contributes to enhance the magic of the boundless "ocean" of sand: the deliberately plain table setting, veil-like curtain and the burbling water reflecting the light add a priceless romantic note to the whole. The setting is the Al Maha Desert Resort.

Left: We are under the eaves of a makuti roof 25 metres high made from interwoven palm leaves and casurina trunks, which only adds to the indescribable spell cast by the African sunset. The place is the west side of the Lion in the Sun Resort, located 70 kilometres from Malindi. The table laid in the European style in no way disturbs the native charm.

IN THE Sun, IN THE Shade

It is a long way from the pavilions of noble country receptions of bygone years to the gazebos and awnings of today's terraces and gardens – but not all that long. Now as in the past, everyone is prepared to shelter company from the blistering sun or drizzle, taking care not to conceal the surrounding beauty. What we do is turn a bit of the outdoors into a room without walls, delightfully devoid of confines and corners.

When it comes to outdoor luncheons or dinners, those in search of a style of their own are free to follow the most varied paths. There are tables that, even though completely laid, vanish into the white of the plaster, blue of the waves, green of the hedges: only the landscape – urban or rural, marine or country – must dominate the aesthetic emotions of the table companions. The tableware provides a discrete aid to the mimesis, adapting to the opaque thickness of the earth and transparency of the air.

Other tables feel like ambassadors of the home outside the house, unwilling to do without place cards, carafe, silverware, decoration or *surtout de table*. Fortunately, nothing is obligatory, above all simplicity.

Lower left: Protagonist, equatorial vegetation. The corner reserved for breakfast in a large villa in the vicinity of Malindi lives is close symbiosis with the colours, shapes and scents of the African nature it is immersed in. "Inside" and "outside" become meaningless notions.

Lower right: India? Maghreb? Where might this outdoor dining room with its pronounced exotic flavour be? Paradoxically, in the countryside of Tuscany. Here time and space expand, joining East and West, tradition and imagination. Around the table iron chairs from India go well with the Moroccan lantern.

Right: Bastide de Marie, dating from the eighteenth century, is a former farmhouse turned into a charming hotel. Immersed in the luxuriant nature of Provence, it gives rise to visions and sensations cherished by the Impressionists. Here one takes an aperitif under the *Bignonia capreolata*, at ease on iron chairs crafted by local artisans. The white, red and rosé Cotes du Lubéron wines are of the house.

Left: The garden of Villa Gamberaia is a perfect example of the art of producing a grand effect using small-scale elements. Its beauty is such that one remains engrossed looking at it and contemplating it. Among camellias and terracotta goddesses, a small table laid for breakfast with aristocratic porcelains seems to partake of so much perfection.

Above: The outdoor dinner at the Geneva villa of major jeweller and designer Fawaz Gruosi includes a round table with green top, a blaze of red roses and a minimal table setting. The true protagonists are the garden and flowered pergola colouring and framing the setting with a striking perspective effect.

Following pages: The summertime garden often becomes a sort of extra room tinted with green. In this Cetona villa in Tuscany near Siena, the luxuriant foliage forms a shady portico where it is a sublime pleasure to dine with rustic plates the colour of water and sturdy glasses for the Chianti. The cat Nelson agrees.

Above: We are in the garden of an Indonesian dwelling where a blend of local and Islamic culture produces suggestive effects. Surrounded by the inebriating scents of the thick equatorial vegetation, a footbridge marked by Arabic lanterns leads to an unusual *en-plein-air dining room*.
A bench tinged with fuchsia rings a table characterised by a small central fountain of Mozarabic inspiration.

Right: Metaphysical *déjeuner sur l'erbe* in a view of the fabulous Italian garden of Villa Gamberaia just outside Florence. We seem to hear the distant voices of children playing ball, whose mothers will soon call them for a snack already waiting; the breeze carries the murmurs of sweethearts in the shade of the trees or topiary hedges.

Left: A table at the Acajou restaurant of the Hotel Sandy Lane, on the West Coast of Barbados, directly overlooks the sea. Lulled by a steady breeze and in setting of refined simplicity, table companions can savour refined seafood dishes while enjoying the unsurpassable spectacle of the crystalline waters of the Caribbean.

Lower left: The large matelassé sofa beds that underline the perimeter of this terrace overlooking the rooftops of Florence afford an unforgettable view of the architectural masterpieces of the city symbolised by the iris. Well-known architect Guido Ciompi designed the painted metal and teak table. The Cheap Chic chairs are by XO.

Lower right: Dawn is breaking over Porto Rotondo. The table on the panoramic terrace is already laid for breakfast with cups and teapot by Surimono. The flooring is natural iroko. Beyond the parapet, the rocking lights of the boats anchored in the snug harbour still shine.

Following pages: Evening falls over Pantelleria. The lanterns are lit in the suggestive dining area of this *dammuso*; the hostess serves her guests, stretched out on comfortable Oriental-style cushions, fragrant mint tea and tasty local specialities, while the nearby stars twinkle. And here the stars are truly at our fingertips.

Above left: At dusk, the *opus incertum terrace affords* a spectacular vista of the Gulf of Tigullio. The table, whose top is enriched by a mosaic with a marine subject, seems lost in time, suspended in a magic setting designed by the sea. The candlesticks are by Do Konig Vassilakis; the table setting is minimal but elegant, leaving room for the emotion of the moment.

Above right: The magic of the evening: the rounded hills of Tuscany are inlaid with a filigree of lights; a steadfast lion watches over the safety of those present. And then the table lit by flickering candles, the elegant table setting.... What is more romantic than dinner on the terrace of Villa Gamberaia?

Right: The setting is practically created from nothing, but how much charm! A deck, two plain wooden armchairs, a Spartan table and the endless blue of the Indian Ocean, even more intense in the light of the lamps that go on when the fiery sun sinks below the horizon. This is what awaits guests of the Four Season Resort of Kuda Hura, Maldives, who dine at the Reef Club. The cuisine features dishes that combine native flavours and Mediterranean recipes.

By Candlelight

Relegated by the coming of electric light to the modest role of substitute during blackouts, the candle is now making a triumphal comeback. Never really vanished from aristocratic dinner tables and an irreplaceable ingredient of a romantic dinner for two, it is regaining favour for public and private occasions, whether in the daytime or in the evening, Franciscan or neo-baroque.

A white taper is a sure road to basic elegance. If we stray a bit from habit, we discover that a candle can also be coloured, twisted, huge, floating, dripping, flower-shaped, like a pastry, with seashells or pebbles or pearls or something else, scented, smokeless.…

But when it comes to shedding gentle light on a table there is nothing better than tall white odourless candles: raised on candlesticks, multiplied by double holders and candelabra, protected by valuable cut and ground crystal. The rays of the warm, flickering flames accentuate the tints of the tableware, brighten the silver. They make wine poured in goblets glimmer darkly.

They caress foods without revealing their material nature. They confine the surrounding environment to the shadows, leaving the table's faint ring of light for meaningful glances. We might be in a picture by Caravaggio or a Dutch interior. We let ourselves go. And we also deceive ourselves. As the old adage goes, *"Né donna né tela a lume di candela."*

The warning is against being taken in by the soft, languid beauty of a face barely glimpsed, no less than the superficial charm of a painting whose particulars and condition are unclear. But aside from not falling in love too fast and avoiding rash art purchases, the aesthetic pleasures aroused by candlelight are the intangible ingredient that heightens the delights of dining together.

Above left: A Mediterranean setting, sunny and rarefied, dominated by the play of the wrought iron and *ton sur ton*: the standout red tabletop rivets attention, lending emphasis to a laying of the dinner table as informal as it is elegant.

Above right: Present and past meet in the dining room of a Lombardy residence. The table is laid with porcelains and a centrepiece recalling the fertility of Nature. Studio Linea designed the chairs covered with white silk; the richly framed charcoal drawing, hung above the chest of drawers dating from the early nineteenth century, is by Renato Guttuso.

Right: The tablecloth may be missing, but not an aristocratic aura: taken as a whole, the candlesticks, crystal goblets, plates by Versace, silver cutlery and tableware, and high-back chairs covered with damask with a flower pattern create a sophisticated patrician atmosphere. Sealing the luxury are a valuable Lombardy canvas with a rural subject and a large urn embellished with plant life in relief.

This is the table of tradition par excellence. Everything speaks of the family, its history and wealth stratified over the centuries, from the small oval portraits of the ancestors to the large mirror, fruitstand with grapes hanging down, candelabra embellishing the table, putti, bisque floral decoration and plates.

An indoor middle-class portrait, one might say, thinking of the dinners narrated by Antonio Fogazzaro.

These pages: Arab-inspired suggestions blend with Old World charms in the dining room of a London dwelling. The opulence of

the fabrics with their warm, deep tones and the comfortable elegance of the furniture give life to rhythms and fragrances recalling

earlier eras. The smooth William IV mahogany table reflects valuable Regency silver.

The dark gold wallpaper, glowing in the candlelight, features Ottoman and Mozarabic writing.

Above: The striking feature of this Engadine home is wood, with the wall panelling producing the convivial feeling of the *stüa*. Without frills, the small seventeenth-century worktable has been converted for dining tête-à-tête, displaying the beauty of simplicity. The leather chairs date from the nineteenth century, as does the painting of flowers by Giuseppe Vicenzino, hung the widow.

Left: The Salle des Gardes restaurant of the Hotel Château de Bagnols near Lyons is organised around a gigantic marble fireplace in flamboyant Gothic style, France's largest, with friezes illustrating the visit of Charles VIII in 1490. The Louis Treize chairs are covered with silk of the period. The restrained elegance of the table setting is in keeping with the feeling of ancient nobility that steeps the environment.

Above: The small drawing room is in a Paris home owned by a cultured traveller and passionate collector. The divan was once a large Louis Seize bed. Etruscan vases inspire the striking black Wedgwood porcelain service on the tray in the foreground.

Right: Franca Sozzani, *Vogue* editor and high priestess of international fashion, treated herself to a house in Marrakech, creatively interpreting the cosmopolitan culture of old Morocco without regard for passing trends. In the darkened dining room she has staged a suggestive setting that successfully blends disparate elements of Jewish civilisation – including a menorah, votive panel and wall decorated with graphic traces – and the Arab world, including the lantern. A few Western touches add to the mix.

Preceding pages: In the new pavilion of Bali's Tugu Hotel there is also a blend of history and culture, things sacred and profane, Indonesia and China: guests enjoy the *peranakan* cuisine mingling Chinese and Dutch flavours, benevolently watched over by Buddha in various guises. An important collection of archaeological findings completes the formal and intellectual refinement of the setting. The work is by Anhar Setjadibrata, *deus ex machina* of every room in the unsurpassable luxury resort.

Above: Walls painted Pompeii red using a special *velatura* finish adorn the dining room walls of a young and dynamic couple in Milan. A seventeenth-century mythological painting of the Bologna school dominates. The mahogany table is enhanced by ethereal crystal candlesticks and a vase centrepiece from Myanmar, with coloured tulips and *Fresia refracta* like a picture by Giuseppe Recco.

Left: "Emotion in Red" might be the name of the dining room of this Paris mansion dating from the days before Napoleon's rise, in view of the dominant colour of the tablecloth, goblets and upholstery, while the drapes mix red and gold. There is something of Matisse in this vivid display that resonates in the cups, fruit bowl, candleholders and other porcelain objects forming the table setting.

Printed in China, July 2008